IN THE GARDEN

IN THE GARDEN

God Speaks

Our time is very special to *you*...
Our time is very special to me *too*...

Belinda F. Payne

ISBN: 978-1-7324670-1-9

Published by Kindle Direct Publishing (KDP)

Subject Heading Religion\Devotional\Poetry

Otherwise noted, all Scripture quotations are from the King James Version® (KJV) of the Holy Bible 1967 Edition of the Scofield Reference Study Bible.

Cover Photo:

Hemant Lal
www.AaronProductionsIndia.com

Dedication

To

Alvin

Trey and Jolea

Jeffrey and Lacy

Kelby and Xander James

Angela and Ashton

In The Garden

The Lord speaks, and the
sound of his voice is so tender and
sweet even the birds hush their singing.

Table of Contents

Acknowledgments · xi
Authors Note · xiii
Introduction ·xv
Prologue · xix

My Grace is Sufficient for Thee... · 1
Grace, Grace, Grace · 3
How Long? · 5
The Struggle · 7
I Don't Know · 9
I Used to Dream... ·10
Wisdom · 12
Father, I Thank You · 15
Because I Love You ·16
Faith ·18
Enduring Faithfulness · 20
Who Am I? · 23
A Broken Heart · 24
Lord Have Mercy ... One More Time · · · · · · · · · · · · · · · · · · · 26
Not Just Another Woman · 28
Submission · 30
Me, Myself and I ·32
Suddenly ·35
God's Will ... What a Strange God · 36
The Voice of God · 38

Is Life Fair? ·41
The Current· 43
The Anger Inside · 45
Goodnight Lord, You Take the Night-Shift· · · · · · · · · · · · · · · 47
In My Room· 49
My Mother's Morning Prayer · 53
Since I Don't Know ·55
Praying God's Word · 57
What about me? What do I Get out of the Deal? · · · · · · · · · · · ·61
Our Special Moments · 65
The Benediction· 67

Acknowledgments

To God, be the glory for every good and perfect work He has chosen to perform in my life. *God, I love you!*

To my mother and father, you will always be the best parents on God's green earth!

To my entire family, who has loved me just the way I am. You have always walked with me and encouraged me to be myself. My love, respect, and admiration for you are immeasurable.

To my friends who have engraved golden memories in my life, thank you for sowing into my life. Each of you has provided me with experiences I will cherish forever. Imprinted in my heart is each encounter, none of which I am not willing to omit. No, not even one!

To my two special friends who took the time to review, critique, and provide feedback, I am humbled and grateful. *Thank you.*

To my prayer partners, we have prayed over a countless number of sensitive and challenging situations for our lives, family, friends, and even strangers. To you, I say, "Iron sharpeneth iron; so a man Sharpeneth the countenance of his friend" (Proverbs 27:17).

To each of you, I dedicate this book. I could never have done it without you.

Authors Note

was baptized as a child and attended a small community Baptist church. I remember singing the old hymn *"In the Garden"* that was written by C. Austin Miles in March 1912. For some strange reason, that familiar chorus rang aloud in my ears throughout my life. This song had special meaning to me at a very early age. Now many years later, I see why I fell in love with the words of that song.

My garden is a sacred, anointed place for special times spent with God. *It is my soul.* When I go to the garden, I find God is always there waiting upon my return. I enter into the very presence of God and experience worship.

My book *In the Garden* bloomed out of my journaling. I began to write down my thoughts, emotions, and experiences many years ago. I dared not share or reveal them to anyone. Now they have become a collection of daily devotions comprised of below the surface, honest talks I had with God. I did not realize God was developing a book within me. These devotions are a daily spiritual supplement designed to encourage open, breathtaking worship with God Almighty.

But now I find God had other plans. You do know that we can plan, but God can *unplan*, don't you? I am ready to reveal all of me to you. Someone I don't know. But you are certainly someone who knows me. You know me because you see yourself in my writing. So, don't be afraid of me. Don't be scared to admit to God that you have felt or experienced some of the same strange thoughts, fears, and emotions I have felt. *Hey*, I guess I do know you!

Take time to establish your routine in meeting with the Lord. Go to *your garden* to be with the Father as often as needed to find the peace, joy, and deliverance you have been longing to receive. *Even if you have fallen away, it's never too late to start over.* God, in His infinite wisdom, designed it that way because God is a God of another chance, for people who need many opportunities. Praise God!

No more masks. No more veils. No more pretending. No more walls. No more excuses. Sure, it's scary, and it is also painful, but it will be worth it. Ask God to meet with you and speak to you above the mercy seat. Ask Him to reveal His hidden truths to you. Then submit yourself under the anointing of God.

If you're not sure how to do that here's a simple prayer:

Lord, I commend my spirit unto you. Take full control of my thoughts. Forgive me of my sins. Fall fresh upon me. Now fill me with your Holy Spirit. Speak Lord. I am listening.

Amen.

Introduction

"*In the Garden*" is an inspirational collection of powerful devotionals. Constantly are we bombarded with disturbing news, but this is a refreshing read. The author, Belinda F. Payne, is a committed believer who has also authored "Sorting Through God's Love." Belinda has very openly and candidly shared what she has heard from God over the years of her life. When we read what God has spoken through this author, we realize it is good news. The God of the universe longs for the opportunity to give us His instructions for an abundant life. We are His highest creation for which He has paid the highest ransom.

This inspired work makes it clear that God has given us the power to influence and impact the quality of life we live by being in God's presence each day. Time with the Father will keep us inspired and give us peace, joy, and deliverance in this fallen world. God will use this particular time to reveal His heart not only for ourselves but for us to demonstrate His love to others. It is He who has made us and not we ourselves, as so eloquently spoken in the Psalm.

In each devotion, she offers the insight she received from scripture, and in her time, In The Garden with the Father. For example, when she leads us through her struggle to understand events happening at a certain point in her life, she references Isaiah 48:18, which provides a scriptural recipe for peace amidst the battle, "Oh, that thou hadst hearkened to my commandments! Then had thy peace been like a river, and thy righteousness like the waves of the sea."

This author transparently and openly discusses some of her most protected and personal thoughts with her readers, and this opens a productive dialogue about what it means to live a life according to God's plan. She explains that even if we are far from the perfect blueprint, God is fully capable of getting us there. It is In The Garden, where those loving conversations with the Father take place, and our movement towards a place of peace begins.

Belinda shows us evidence of God's love, even when our behavior is less than perfect. She further shows us that God longs to direct our paths that will lead us to His master plan and purpose specifically designed for our lives. God is not a respecter of persons, and by deduction, we can say with certainty that what He has done in the author's life, he will do for us. He is immutable, the same God today, yesterday and forever.

When given a choice, most of us will choose the option of least input and the highest output. However, in spiritual matters, we understand that God seeks a heart that is inclined to His ways, and He expects that we will serve Him with our whole heart. In no uncertain terms, this author helps her readers to understand that God desires an intimate relationship with each of us. Maintaining this intimate relationship is not a solo undertaking; instead, it requires input from both you and God. No matter where you are in your relationship continuum at the time of reading this insightful devotional, you will be inspired to take your walk with God to a higher level. The benefits will be worth every effort made to establish a regular time of fellowship with God, who loves you more than anyone. So, I encourage you to approach your intake of its content with vigor and to look for God to reciprocate.

As one whose commitment to the Lord is established, I read this soul-searching account of God's love for me, and I am inspired to elevate my worship time with Him. Many of the experiences cited in the collection of devotionals resonated with me, and I am sure some will resonate with you as well. The rich reward of spending time with God far outweighs any sacrifice you or I may be required to make. Let us not act in a manner of just "checking a box" but rather let us enter into His courts with expectation, thanksgiving, and praise.

If you want to increase your knowledge of God, improve your prayer outcomes, and strengthen your walk with God, this powerful devotional will help you get there. Prepare to be blessed.

Many lives will be blessed through this tremendous work. To God, be the glory.

Annetta Culver, Southern Illinois

Prologue

Now go, write it before them on a tablet, and note it in a book,
that it may be for the time to come forever and ever.

ISAIAH 30:8

·HIS GRACE·

My Grace is Sufficient for Thee...

I once was young, but now I am older. It feels like I've been on this road of life far longer than my age. Maturation is a never-ending process. My college days and experiences seemed like the best years. That's where I got to know me. What I did not know but later understood was my life was beginning. I had no idea what lay ahead. I had so many dreams and ideas of what I thought life would be like once I emerged from the not-so-real world of college campus living. As life went on, I realized I had bundled up within myself emotions and wounds from battles fought in my mind that I thought were too difficult for me or anyone else to conquer. God began to move in areas of my life; I believed unconquerable. At times, I was utterly overwhelmed at other times, confused. God began to develop a discontent for the superficial within me and created a more deep-seated desire for a spiritual walk within me. This walk would keep me in touch with my soul. *I have learned life is short, so don't waste time on needless things.*

Eventually, everyone will come to the point of soul-searching and self-realization. However, humbling that may sound, my tests, trials, and tribulations continued to pour in. God began to confront me with my very own burning bushes. I cannot count the times I faced burning bushes in my pathway. As I look back, I saw I turned back, or I chose to go around my burning bushes, never stopping long enough to listen to the voice of God for instructions. I did not understand there would be times in which I would have to pass through the fire. I discovered later that even if God allowed it, He never planned for me to get burned.

You cannot begin to understand how much time I have wasted. Perhaps I would be further along in life had I stopped to listen to God's voice. Maybe I wouldn't have gotten scorched by the fire so many times had I obeyed God. I worked hard to be what I thought others wanted me to be, never listening to find out what God designed me to be. I was so self-determined that I almost came face to face with self-destruction — good intentions but not obedient. You understand, don't you? *I struggled.* Jesus took my struggles before the Father and interceded on my behalf. Jesus showed me His mercy. His *grace* is beyond measure. *That's when I entered into His rest.*

Prayer: Lord, teach me the spiritual principles that govern my life. Help me to understand You will not always change my conditions. But that does not mean You don't care. It means You have a more excellent plan that I cannot see. May my heart and mind reflect You. One of the most magnificent words of encouragement You have given me when I do not understand Your plan is, "My grace is sufficient for you." As I pray and look back over my life, I realize it is.

> *And he said unto me, My grace is sufficient for thee: for my strength is made perfect in weakness. Most gladly therefore will I rather glory in my infirmities, that the power of Christ may rest upon me.*

> 2 CORINTHIANS 12:9

Grace, Grace, Grace

t's not a cliché. *It is the truth!* Where would we be if it were not for God's grace? There are so many things I could say about His grace to try to inspire you. But only God can inspire you with and by His grace. That which God does in response to our prayers is a result of His grace. *The provisions He releases is all about grace.* Even when He chooses not to change our circumstances, it is still evidence of His unmerited favor towards us. God's favor, we do not deserve, and we have no way to earn it.

He does not rewrite the hands of time. He does not always rid us of our enemies. *Howbeit, He chooses to bestow His blessing upon us in the presence of our enemies.* He gives us a massive dose of His grace, and by this, we know He loves us. Why would you need any more than that?

Prayer: God, I thank You for your kindness and graciousness towards humanity without regard to works or merit. It is an expression of Your unconditional love. It is the essence of Your love in the likeness of Christ, Your Son. I realize Your grace is the sustenance You provide in response to our prayers. I accept and receive Your bountiful provision of grace.

> *Many, O Lord my God, are thy wonderful works which thou hast done, and thy thoughts which are to us-ward; they cannot be reckoned up in order unto thee: If I would declare and speak of them, they are more than can be numbered.*

PSALMS 40:5

3

·I DON'T·
UNDERSTAND

How Long?

Take it from someone who knows. Obedience will always outweigh sacrificial rituals. As children, we learn to share. But there is a nature that rises very early in the heart of a child, and one of the first words assimilated is "no." *We enter into this world rebelling against all forms of teaching that tell us self-denial and submission is the way to exaltation.* Then we begin to ask the question, *"How long?"* How long will it be before I am successful? Well, I can answer that. That's up to you and me. *It all depends on how many times we get in the way.* Sometimes life requires self-denial through submission of one's self to others, and that is when the battle begins. *Battles begin and end in the mind.* The carnal mind will always choose itself over others because flesh and blood are all about self-gratification. In a world that defines success based upon one's individuality and unique perceptions of success, you may find yourself struggling to understand this concept of self-denial and submission. Each day you rise, you must face the challenges and demands others place upon you. These demands often require that you place the need of others above your own. Are you faced with putting your dreams on hold? If so, you understand what I mean.

To fulfill our pleasure is not why God created us. Serving others is our purpose. Do you live by the philosophy of, it's my way or no-way? The only way to change-is-to-change. Change the way you see yourself by looking at yourself through the eyes of others. Be willing to see what others see in you. That includes the good, the bad, and the ugly. Overcome selfishness. Commit to looking for opportunities to serve others with your gifts and talents.

Many people spend their entire life searching for joy and fulfillment in all the wrong places, only to end life, never having experienced it in its abundance and all its splendor. I have discovered through my children that life is precious. *Life is a gift.* You have a season of time to live, achieve, and accomplish all that God has designed for you. How long? *It's, however, long it takes for the revelation of the manifestation of who you are in all your greatness coupled with all your weakness to become a realization to you.* That's how long!

Prayer: Oh my Lord, I do not want to be the one in which it takes a lifetime to learn how to live; I want to be free in You. You brought me into this earth with a purpose to bring You glory by what I say and do. I am tired of looking for fulfillment in and through the eyes and life of others. Please show me how to seek You for the answers and direction I need. I repent for being a selfish and self-centered person. Please forgive me and show me how to serve You by serving others.

And when he had called the people unto him with his disciples also, he said unto them, Whosoever will come after me, let him deny himself, and take up his cross, and follow me.

MARK 8:34

The Struggle

*H*ow do you let go? How do you make yourself stop thinking about it over and over again? After we have toiled and wrestled with the cares of this life, we often find that not only have we exhausted all possibilities for a solution to our problem, but we have exhausted ourselves mentally, physically, and spiritually as well. Somehow, we fail to understand all we had to do was let go. Our heavenly Father is prepared to handle it. *I did not know that I can never fix what was wrong or make what was wrong, right.* I felt my life was in a quandary. My heart and mind were overwhelmed because I was not trusting God.

I decided to make a prayer box. I listed everything that concerned me on tiny sheets of paper and placed them in my new prayer box. I took this box into my hands and lifted it in the air and presented it to God.

Prayer: Father, I thank and bless Your Holy Name. I love and exalt You. You are Almighty. I know You are more than capable of handling everything written on these slips of paper. I give every issue, name, and condition to You. I am casting all my cares upon You because I believe in my heart you care for me. I leave all my concerns at Your feet. I release my pain and my struggles into Your mighty hands. I know You will work everything out for my good because I love You, and I am one of those called of You, and I walk in Your purpose for my life.

Oh, that thou hadst hearkened to my commandments! Then had thy peace been like a river, and thy righteousness like the waves of the sea.

Isaiah 48:18

I Don't Know

"*I don't know if I can trust You again.*" There, I said it. It's not that I don't believe in Your power. I've seen You work in the lives of others. I even know Your mighty hand has been keeping and protecting my life. *But this is different.* Now You ask me to trust You at an even higher level. *You ask me to trust Your love for me*, but I've never really experienced Your love before. I don't know You. That's my issue!

The only way to know God is to spend time with God. God expresses His love for us in and through the experiences; we encounter in our lives. Some of these experiences bring us unspeakable joy, while others cloaked in unbearable pain and sorrow bring despair. Knowing God on the surface or based solely upon a song or, according to someone else's testimony, will never be enough to sustain you when you face turbulent times. Not only will you need to know you trust God at all times, but God also needs to know you trust Him at all times.

Prayer: Oh, Lord, my God, it is so important to me that I know You. I need You to be my fortress and my deliverer. Bless me to be free to experience a loving relationship with You. Bless me to know You and the power of Your love.

> *The Lord is good, a stronghold in the day of trouble, and he knoweth those who trust in him.*

> Nahum 1:7

I Used to Dream...

I used to dream. *I used to hope. I used to believe. I used to have visions.* I would love to dream, hope, believe, and have visions again. However, fear and the collisions of life have taken their toll on me. *Instead, I have learned to hide.* Hide all my worries and my dreams. You see, sometimes dreams don't come true, and the pain can be unbearable. *But life without dreams is no life at all.* Rejection can be heartbreaking. For many years I dreamed of writing a book. I would submit my work time after time, only to have my submissions rejected. With each denial, my hope waivered. My vision of becoming a published author dimmed. I felt like a sunken ship at sea. I stopped sharing my dream with others for fear of mockery and scorn. I am so grateful God never gave up on me. The Holy Spirit quickened me never to give up! I gave my dream another chance. You are reading it right now; *#inpursuitofmydreams* became my reality.

My confession to God was that I was finally ready to live, dream, hope, and have visions again. *However painful it may be to begin again, I am ready. The confidence inside of me is far greater than my fears opposing me. I used to fear.*

Prayer: Father of all creation, I am a dreamer. But somewhere along the way, I lost my zeal and passion. You have placed Your gifts and talents within me, and I let them go dormant. I ask You to restore the intense Spirit that was once there and ignite my passion for pursuing all my dreams.

According to my earnest expectation and my hope, that in nothing I shall be ashamed, but that with all boldness, as always, so now also Christ shall be magnified in my body, whether it be by life or by death.

Philippians 1:20

Wisdom

There will always be stones in our path; some are smooth and beautiful, while others are grey, jagged, and sharp. We must identify every stone in our footpath. I have learned it is crucial to keep our spiritual senses in a *ready mode*. That does not mean we must live life on the edge; it means we must be *prepared* and *alert*. Some stones you shall innocently stumble upon and fall. Deliberately thrown are some stones in your way as a means to discourage you.

You will be able to kick some stones out of our path. It will be necessary for you to recognize other stones are there for you to stand upon and make you spiritually taller, enabling you to rise above your circumstances.

God has given us His Spirit of Wisdom to instruct, protect, and guide us during times of opposition and struggle. Those who rise to the level of being called wise have learned to use life's tests as stepping-stones instead of stumbling blocks.

I have missed the Lord on many occasions because I did not seek His Wisdom while on my stony path. Not only should I have done so for essential decisions but the simple choices as well. It is God's pleasure to guide us into all truth. It is His to offer and ours to receive or reject.

Prayer: Oh my God, I don't understand why I keep tripping and falling. Why are there so many stones in my path? Why do I keep making the same mistakes? When I look at things, they appear one way on the outside only to learn things are not what they appear to be. I need You to lead me beside still waters. Take these stumbling blocks out of my way. Give me your Spirit of Wisdom, so I have discernment. Give me clarity, so I understand what is before me. I desire to do the right thing. Protect me from those that can potentially harm me as I learn to hear and obey Your voice.

> *Then I saw that wisdom excelleth folly,*
> *as far as light excelleth darkness.*

Ecclesiastes 2:13

SO GRATEFUL

Father, I Thank You

I experienced such freedom once I became fully aware there wasn't anything I could ever do to make God love me more, nor could I impress Him with my works. Hence, I decided I would stop doing things I saw other people do that I interpreted as being significant in the eyes of God. *Those actions were outside of my nature and character anyway. God never intended for me to be like anyone else.* That was all my doing. I was so silly to think that. Once I learned all I had to do was love God with all my heart, everything else began to flow freely. Without my beckoning, God planted within me the seed of a worshiper. Then He birthed within me the heart of a worshiper. That became one of my greatest delights!

Prayer: Jehovah God, I trust You, to live Your life through me. I no longer place any value on keeping rules and regulations to be accepted and loved by You. I recognize this is sin, and You would never require this of me. Your Son's blood has purchased me. I am free from the bondage of the law of sin and death. Father, I thank You for accepting me as I am and for acknowledging me as Your child. Lord, I want to be so in love with You today and each day forever. I am willing to express my love for You by stepping out in faith this day. Out of the bondage of works, I emerge into a life of grace. My conduct will be a representation of my love for You. Not because I have to. It's just because I love You. Thank You for loving me just the way I am.

We love him, because he first loved us.

I John 4:19

Because I Love You

have this issue about hiding things! When I was a child, my grandma would come from out-of-state to visit. I often hid her belongings because I did not want my grandma to leave and stay at the home of her siblings during her visit. I did not want to share her with anyone, not even her brothers and sisters, who longed to see her. I hoped by hiding her sweater; it would permanently delay her departure. I wanted her all to myself. Then I moved on to trying to hide my presence from others. Many times, I entered a crowded room; I wanted to go unnoticed. I would find a secluded space to hide. I once hid in the backseat floorboard of my uncle's car so that I could go with him. Oh my, did I get in trouble for that one! *Once upon a time, I also hid God's presence in my life, so others would not know I was one of His.*

How do you tell Your heavenly Father, you're sorry? Lord, as I look back over my life, I see how I have hurt You. By blocking Your love, resisting, and quenching Your presence. I have hidden Your spiritual gifts, burying them within me instead of using them to bless others. What father would not hurt if his child ashamedly rejected his love and his gifts over and over again?

Prayer: I confess to You, my Father, that You have loved me with an unconditional love that has no beginning and has no end. Yes, You have remained right here. Even when I did not know how to receive Your love, You remained faithful to me. You cradled me in Your loving arms as only a father could. Now I will love You, freely, openly, and unashamed as *my* heavenly Father and *my* God.

> *Praise ye the Lord, I will praise the Lord with my whole heart,*
> *in the assembly of the upright, and in the congregation.*

PSALMS 111:1

Faith

often struggled as I grew in Christ. I questioned; how do I have faith? How do I know if I have it or not when it is intangible? When will I know if I have enough faith to please God? My human desire longed for physical proof. The Holy Spirit taught me there is no single answer to any of these perplexing questions. *One thing is sure; the level of faith that worked the last time did not work the next time.* What I needed was a new faith for every unique experience because each experience was a new journey.

Abraham never doubted. His faith and trust grew stronger, and he learned to praise God in advance. God operates differently than a man. Because of your faith, God will bring you into a place of highest privilege where you can stand confidently and joyfully looking forward to becoming all that God has destined you to be. Therefore, rejoice when you come into trials and temptations. These trials help you to develop patience. Patience develops the strength of one's character as you learn to trust God more and more. As a result, your faith will be strong and steady. According to your faith, the Holy Spirit maketh intercession for you. For you don't know what to pray for as you should, but He will pray to the Father fervently, with words that cannot be expressed by mere man.

Prayer: Heavenly Father, I confess I do not know what to pray. I know that You know my heart. I need Your Holy Spirit, who knows my heart to make intercession for me. I know the Holy Spirit will present my case before You. Oh my goodness, I am so grateful the Holy Spirit pleads for me in harmony with Your will. I do not want to continue to walk after the flesh. I want to live by faith. Supernaturally anoint me with Your Holy oil. Thank You for empowering me to keep going. Yea, by faith, I decree and declare I will praise You in advance for those things, which are not, as though they be.

...but the just shall live by faith.

HABAKKUK 2:4b

Enduring Faithfulness

Enduring faithfulness is an expression of our unconditional love for God. *Through our trials, God uses the ultimate and most effective tool, "the trial itself," to strengthen our faith and produce enduring faithfulness*

And yes, as much as we may not like it, the trial is the evidence of Jehovah Shammah's presence with us. We have infallible proof He has not forsaken or abandoned us. *If we are careful not to interrupt the process, we shall come forth mature and complete - perfect in Christ, having learned how to focus on who He is and not what He does for us.*

God never promised us life would be easy. He told us a man that is born of a woman is of a few days, and we should anticipate those days, shall be full of trouble. *Do not fret. Be of good cheer.* God has already equipped His children with everything they need to be an overcomer.

Prayer: Lord, release within me Your Spirit of Wisdom. Give me the strength to endure with a faithful heart. I do not want to be a quitter. Let endurance have its perfect work. I desire to emerge from every trial with a greater love for You, the giver of all life, than for life itself.

> *Persecutions, afflictions, which came unto me at Antioch, at Iconium, at Lystra, what persecutions I endured; but out of them all the Lord delivered me. Yea, and all that will live godly in Christ Jesus shall suffer persecution.*

> 2 TIMOTHY 3:11-12

·BUT I'M·
STILL
CONFUSED

Who Am I?

I represent three people at all times, no matter where I go. *I am me, myself, and I.* I am confident, secure, and intelligent full of self-respect, sensitivity, integrity, and human dignity. I am the apple of God's eye. I do not need to compete with anyone to be like anyone. God's hands fearfully and wonderfully made me. God designed me to be who I am, and He desires that I love being myself.

Prayer: Jehovah, I am so glad You made me just the way I am. I don't have to work to be or look like anyone else to seek their approval. My mind is sharp. I belong to You, Lord. Take all of these influences and turn them into something useful that may benefit the kingdom. When You look upon my countenance, I pray You will see a reflection of You.

> *Lo, children are an heritage from the Lord; and the fruit of the womb is his reward. Happy is the man who hath his quiver full of them.*

PSALMS 127:3,5a

A Broken Heart

A broken heart. Who can trust it? Who can know it? Who can understand it? I have dealt with people who have a broken heart. Sometimes they are unreachable and inconsolable. I recall the last days of my father's illness with cancer when the hospice caseworker advised us not to make any rash decisions or significant changes in our lifestyle once he had transitioned. That seemed rather odd as his absence itself would change everything we knew about our lifestyle. But the focus was on those that remained not on those who were moving on to eternity. *The reality was choices are for the living.* Her experience was that many people who lose a loved one are unable to use sound judgment to make wise choices because they make decisions out of a broken heart. They often look back months or years later with regret. We serve a God who searches the heart and tests our conscience and rewardeth every man according to his ways and the motives of his own soul. There is no need to wonder if God knows and understands the brokenness you are feeling. The heart shall be broken and shattered into many fragmented pieces. But our God specializes in picking up the pieces and putting it back together, *and He shall give you a new heart.*

Prayer: Father of light and life I ask You to protect my broken heart, so I mitigate my risk of becoming vulnerable to the prey lurking around, seeking to devour me. Shine Your light onto my dark path. Illuminate my mind so that I understand the changes going on around me and inside of me. Thank You for holding me close to Your bosom as I go through my transition.

Search me, O God, and know my heart; try me, and know my thoughts; And see if there be any wicked way in me, and lead me in the way everlasting.

PSALMS 139:23-24

Lord Have Mercy ...
One More Time

One thing is sure, repeatedly making the same mistake is painful. Failing to learn from dysfunctional backward ways of thinking held me back from achieving promotions and recognitions. It also caused me to live in captivity way too long. It wasn't until I made up my mind to get rid of that old nature that my future changed for the better. Each time this negative way of thinking tried to resurface; I took dominion over my thoughts. I put myself in check. I stamped those unwelcome thoughts under my feet. Was it easy? No. Can it be done? Yes.

Prayer: Master, You allowed me the opportunity to prove my love and faithfulness amid adversity. But I failed the test *one more time.* As soon as the calamity struck, I retreated to my old nature. Please forgive me for my iniquities and transgressions. I neglected to commune with You daily. Oh Lord! Have mercy on me for I have sinned...*one more time.* Grant me Your power to quickly recognize when I am falling back into my old ways. Help me, to be honest with myself, for this is the only way I will defeat this behavior and stop this cycle of doing and saying the wrong thing that leads me back into captivity.

The Lord is merciful and gracious, slow to anger, and plenteous in mercy. He will not always chide; neither will he keep his anger forever. He hath not dealt with us after our sins, nor rewarded us according to our iniquities.

PSALMS 103:8-10

Not Just Another Woman

was enlightened and inspired after reading the book of Esther in the Old Testament. I thought, *wow*, no one knew Esther – she was just an ordinary woman. There was nothing remarkable about her. She did not stand out in the crowd. But there was something powerful brewing on the inside of her. *She was invaluable to the Kingdom of God. She had been anointed and appointed by God without her knowledge or consent.* The spiritual birth that would take place was soon to be known by all. I realized the same applied to me. *Unbeknown* to me, the blueprint and tapestry of my life were being woven each day with every breath I took. I learned every person would have a *"such a time as this"* moment. God will receive glory through it.

So even if I may go unnoticed in the world of the rich and famous, who's to say that I'm just another woman? You see being, "not just another woman" involves more than being a member of the female gender. It takes time to cultivate a woman's character, self-worth, and self-esteem. It means exposing our weaknesses and faults yet maintaining our integrity. It means promoting our strengths through an attitude of humility.

Prayer: Lord, I praise You. Mighty God, thank You. I possess priceless, precious experiences, and memories that could only have emanated from Your plans for my life. These experiences have shown me it takes unveiling *"the-me-nobody-knows"* and *"the-me-I-don't-want-anybody-to-know"* as part of how You had already ordained to bless me before the beginning of time. The memory of those experiences continually serves to remind me that being "not just another woman" mandates that I must make unpopular decisions, and it may require great self-sacrifices, but each will be well worth it. Thank You for helping me understand this principle. Now I know when a woman discovers her place, this is where she will find inner peace and declare, "I'm not just another woman."

> *And who knoweth whether thou art come to the kingdom for such a time as this? ...and so will I go in unto the king, which is not according to the law. And if I perish, I perish.*

ESTHER 4: 14b, 16b

Submission

Have you ever awakened one day with great exasperation? You found yourself saying, "finally, I have arrived at the state of total exhaustion, frustration, and confusion. I have made myself miserable, and I learned how to make others around me miserable, *I guess I'm happy.*" Well, if you have not said it, I'd be willing to bet someone else has spoken it about you because you have made their life miserable.

There you sit baffled and amazed that anyone would ever think such a thing of you. After all, you have drawn a map of success for your life. Your dreams are a reality. Life is good. The portrait you have drawn for your life only illustrates how far away you are from experiencing happiness, inner peace, joy, and a victorious lifestyle.

It's futile to create *your* definition and paint *your* picture of what *you* or the world portrays as the perfect life, only to find nothing can be further from the truth. But now your life is in disarray. You ask yourself, how you got so far off track trying to be "a-wannabe" but never arriving. Long-suffering is not part of your belief system. *Even though you are hurting, you refuse to live a life of submission under the authority of God.* Yet, you continue to believe all you need is a strong determination and self-will to make it in life. In every person's life, the rain will fall. God requires submission for all.

Prayer: Father, with great exasperation, I awoke. You opened my spiritual eyes. I realized I hadn't made it at all! I acknowledge I do not know how to live a life of submission. I do not even want to live a life of surrender. But my spirit man says yes! Order my steps in Your word, dear Lord. I humbly submit myself under Your full control. I trust You for my future.

I returned, and saw under the sun, that the race is not to the swift, nor the battle to the strong, neither yet bread to the wise, nor riches to men of understanding, nor yet favor to men of skill; but time and chance happeneth to them all.

ECCLESIASTES 9:11

Me, Myself and I

I believe - God is all-powerful; Jesus Christ is God's son; God has a special love for His people. But somehow, I have never thought He loved me for me or that I was significant to Him. So, I disciplined me, very skillfully, and with great diligence not to expect very much attention from God or anyone else. *I doubted anyone could love me just the way I am.*

Somehow, I turned this whole spiritual relationship upside-down. I did not understand God's expressions of love. I thought His gifts were the expression of His love for me. I assumed my work would ignite His passion for me. Indeed, I would never be beautiful enough to be loved in my unsophisticated state.

So, I began a long quest to be like others who I perceived to be extraordinary to God. I began to work harder, hoping I would earn God's favor and His love. Eventually, God opened my spiritual eyes and ears. I was wrong all along. *I had always been the beloved of God.* I also came to realize I was precious to those around me. He changed my disposition and my heart. He filled me with His joy, love, and peace. Now I love being me, myself, and I!

Prayer: Oh my God, this is so difficult for me to confess to You and myself. You already know I worked strategically to bury those thoughts and feelings of inferiority and low self-esteem. I have wasted so much time searching to find the perfect person to model my life after. After reading this entry, now I know I am fearfully and wonderfully made. Even before

You formed me in my mother's womb, You knew me, and You sanctified me and ordained that I glorify Your name in spirit and truth. I repent for trying to find others to replace You. I will look to You as my model.

> *But, now thus saith the Lord who created thee, O Jacob, and he who formed thee, O Israel, Fear not; for I have redeemed thee, I have called thee by thy name; thou art mine.*

Isaiah 43:1

IF I COULD JUST HEAR HIS VOICE

Suddenly

Praise be unto God for His demonstrative love that prepares us for His divine will. *In a moment, in the twinkling of an eye, a "suddenly" experience enters into our lives without warning or permission.* Suddenly we face news we are not prepared to hear; destruction, disappointment, despair, and yes, sometimes grief. But God is an awesome, powerful, and wonderful God. The light of all of this is that we should position ourselves to hear God's voice. God will bring forth His Word to comfort and guide us. God will open our understanding to His will, and we will experience His power and righteousness overflowing.

Prayer: Abba, Father, my life is in Your hands. I give my family and my dear friends to You. I pray for Your blood covering over each one of us. I admit I do not like the thought of these "suddenly" experiences. I need You to teach me how to search for You in everything I experience, whether good or bad. You are sovereign. Please be with me and show me Your loving kindness. I know that if I desire to know You in the fellowship of Your suffering, that means I will face "suddenly" experiences in my own life. Oh, my Father, I need Thee! Please hold me tightly to Your bosom as You carry me through this season.

> *I will instruct thee and teach thee in the way which thou shalt go; I will guide thee with mine eye.*

> PSALMS 32:8

God's Will ... What a Strange God

"**A**nd though the Lord give you the bread of adversity and the water of affliction…". Oh, my goodness, why would this even be in the Bible? Yes, in Isaiah 30:20. I once told the Lord, "Sometimes I don't understand Your love. Sometimes I don't understand Your ways. Sometimes I don't understand Your purpose. Honestly, sometimes I plain don't understand You! Lord, I know You love me, and You desire your best for me. You created me in Your image, and I am from a royal priesthood. I am the seed of the righteous. So, I guess that's why I don't understand. If I am all that, why do You allow me to suffer? I do know that I trust You with all my heart, and I have purposed not to lean unto my understanding. Lord, You promised me You would be my teacher, so why don't I get it?"

The end of that verse says, "yet shall not thy teachers be removed into a corner anymore, but thine eyes shall see thy teachers." What I did not understand then, but I understand now is that God was reassuring me He would reveal this mystery to me. He wanted me to know that He would teach me, and I would see Him in my circumstances with my own eyes. Years have passed by, and the Lord has taught me what all this means as I ate the bread of adversity, and I drank water from the streams of affliction. I had so many questions. I found myself crying out to God, asking, why did "it" have to be this way? I often cried, "Are you going to help me?" "How is all this going to work out?" "Why does it take so long?" *Many questions. Few answers.* Yet, He did instruct me. He did allow me to see Him in every circumstance. But seeing things in a new light was a new thing. It meant processing the details of my experience in the Spirit and not through my emotions. *Now, this was a breakthrough moment for me!* This revelation is what lifted my countenance. My whole perspective changed when I took my eyes off my circumstances and looked at things through God's eyes. *God did not seem strange or appear unloving to me anymore. He just looked like my Father. He just looked like He loved me.*

Prayer: Abba, Father, Your all-consuming love is more vast than my mind and heart can comprehend. It is untouchable, yet I feel its touch all over me. It is difficult to understand, yet You make it so understandable that even a child can comprehend and embrace it. Thank You for teaching me to look at all my circumstances with my spiritual eyes and to listen with my spiritual ears. *It hurts too much when I try to reason Your love with my mind and not my heart.* You have said we must worship You in Spirit and truth. The only way we will ever be able to embrace Your love is through the Holy Spirit. Lord, fill me with Your Holy Spirit. Release within me Your Spirit of Wisdom, Knowledge, Understanding, Counsel, and Might, and by all means, don't leave out clarity and discernment, so I know how to apply each.

> *He is the Rock, his work is perfect; for all his ways are justice; a God of truth and without iniquity, just and right is he.*

> DEUTERONOMY 32:4

The Voice of God

For many years I yearned to know what it would be like to hear the Lord's voice. Would I hear an audible voice, or would it be a sense His presence? Would I feel the touch of his hand? Will I know how and when to listen for it? How will I know it's not my voice or the voice of the enemy? What I had to comprehend was that God would never crash or break in to speak. God will never compete with anything or anyone to talk. He requires our full attention. *If I wanted to know what His voice sounded like, I would first have to understand who He is.* I came to realize God longs to spend time with us. He desires that we separate ourselves from everyone and everything else, enter into that secret place, realizing He will be there waiting upon our arrival. His voice is soft as the morning dew. Yet His voice is firm and seemingly at times without passion. God *is* full of compassion for His people. It is amazingly comforting, giving us assurance and security. At other times it breaks us down but never abandoning. It builds us up, yet makes us humble. The voice of God is always tender and full of mercy.

Prayer: Oh, Lord, none can address our state like You. There is none like You, Lord, with only one voice You speak softly and sweetly to Your beloved. Please teach me to recognize Your voice just as I remember the sound of my earthly father and mother, even in the crowds. I know their voice above all other fathers and mothers who are all around me. Lord speak to me in ways that I understand. Open my ears and my eyes that I may hear You. Remove all the other voices of distraction! Speak Lord, for thy servant heareth.

*And he said, Go forth, and stand upon the mount before the
Lord. And, behold, the Lord passed by, and a great and strong
wind rent the mountains, and broke in pieces the rocks before
the Lord; but the Lord was not in the wind. And after the
wind an earthquake; but the Lord was not in the earthquake.
And after the earthquake a fire; but the Lord was not in the
fire. And after the fire a still, small voice.*

1 Kings 19:11-12

I SURRENDER

Is Life Fair?

Is life fair? How do you define it? Is it when everything lines up in your favor? Is it when everyone agrees with you? When you were a child, were you the one that never played fair, or are you the one that always cried saying they're not playing fair?" Isn't it funny you're still the same way today? Are you the one that says, "I don't see how they got the job!" in bitterness? Are you the one who cheated your way into the promotion? Do you realize you didn't get that way overnight? You were the same way when you were a child. *If you are reading this message, that means there is hope for you and the opportunity for change.*

There's one thing about change, you like change or you don't. Some people run towards change while others run as far away from change as they can get. But change is good. You may be thinking it's the other person that needs to change. *That's the problem!* Stop focusing on what everybody else needs to do and start focusing on what you need to do and what is within your power to change.

The first step is to admit *you* are in the wrong place. The second step is to make a conscious decision to move towards the center of the spiritual continuum that will rebirth the presence of God in you. Both are necessary to have a healthy conscience. Next, identify opportunities for change that promote inner peace and well-being. Believe it or not, God will present these opportunities to you each day. Most people miss their chances due to preconceived ideas of what they allow others to define as an opportunity. Some people lose out because they reject the vessel in which the opportunity comes. Choose to do just the opposite of what you have so meticulously trained yourself to do that set you in your downward spiral. Make a conscious decision not to succumb to the temptation to do things according to your old ways.

You like "you" the way you are, so this is no easy feat. Choose an accountability partner that will require you to keep your goals and push you to excel. Be sure to select someone not afraid to tell you the truth about yourself. Be prepared as this will unmask your negative attitude or behavior and bring it to your level of awareness. Be determined to address and harness these outbursts. When you see this negative behavior rearing its ugly head, stamp it under your feet.

Prayer: God, You are all-powerful. You are the only one that can genuinely manage my unruly ways. I do not embrace change when I do not initiate it. I realize I do not live on an island. I live and work around other human beings. I need the help of the Holy Spirit, and I ask You to give me an accountability partner to keep me in check. I know I am not easy to get along with, but I want to do better. Please help me to change so that You are pleased with my attitude and my behavior.

I can do all things through Christ which strengtheneth me.

PHILIPPIANS 4:13

The Current

I have learned life has a way or running circles around you. If you choose to stand still to rest, you must not rest too long because the currents of life are strong, and drifting is inevitable. There were times in which I was tired, and even though I thought I was moving, it turns out I was only drifting. I learned the hard way that when you drift forward at a snail's pace, many blessings will pass by you. I missed out on great blessings. Drifting backward is not optional. After all, when you go back to your old ways, it is as a dog who returns to lap up his vomit.

Please tell me how in the world could that ever be nourishment for the soul. *Seriously!* Is that what you want to do? Being indecisive is not any better. You can't be all over the place. One day it's yes, the next day it is no, the day after that it is maybe. Oh my goodness! Just make up your mind already. Stop drifting; the confusion will cease. Move *forward* with *purpose*. Learn to hang in there. I learned to press through all that which was opposing my efforts. I chose to "press toward the mark for the prize of the high calling of God in Christ Jesus." Then I made it back to shore safe and sound.

Prayer: Jesus, there are times I want not to shout but holler aloud, "Stop this world and let me off!". I don't want to face these problems and issues anymore. But a small voice within me speaks to me and quickens me to fight against these pessimistic and wayward currents that try to overtake me. Lord God empower me to stay at the helm. Show me how to fight like a good soldier. My life is worth fighting for! Yes, it's night right now, but I know joy comes in the morning. The sun will shine again. Your anointing has taken hold of me and will not let me give up. Help me find my place of spiritual solidarity in which I can construct a new foundation that will be able to withstand the forces of time for the balance of my days.

That we henceforth be no more children, tossed
to and fro, and carried about with every wind of doctrine,
by the sleight of men, and cunning craftiness,
by which they lie in wait to deceive.

Ephesians 4:14

The Anger Inside

There is so much life in anger. It is vibrant and energetic. It is also usually uncontrolled, untamed, and volatile, ready to explode upon impact. God created this emotion called anger. He did not make a mistake. Learning to harness it can be quite a challenge. Otherwise, it will control and enslave you. Sometimes we are angry for not allowing ourselves to become all we can be, for not doing all we are capable of doing and reaching the heights we are capable of attaining. Other times we are completely bewildered and have no idea why we are angry. Anger always has a root buried deep within.

When we grow in Christ, The Holy Spirit teaches us how to sort out our anger to produce a peaceful outcome that will be pleasing to the Father. God develops within us a spirit of humility. When you submit unto God, He will show you why you are angry. God will teach us how to manage both our anger and our pain as we release our will and accept God's will for our lives.

To be angry at the world is merely a reflection of the anger at and with oneself.

Don't be angry with me, angry one.

Prayer: Most powerful God, as I stand in front of this mirror and behold the reflection that I see show me how not to live a life of anger, bitterness, and resentment. Teach me not to be angry at me or to feed the uncontrollable passion inside of me. I only want to experience positive anger that drives me to become angry enough to purpose within myself to overcome my self-debilitating emotions. Lord, I lay all my rage at Your feet. Give me peace. Let me know You and the power of Your might is there to deliver me from me.

> *Create in me a clean heart, O God, and renew a right spirit within me. Restore unto me the joy of thy salvation, and uphold me with a willing spirit.*

> PSALMS 51:10-11

> *Do not be quickly provoked in your spirit, for anger resides in the lap of fools.*

> ECCLESIASTES 7:9

Goodnight Lord, You Take the Night-Shift

I knew there was no sense in both God and me staying awake all night dealing with my problems. I remember crying out to God, "Lord, never forget Your promises to me for they gird my loins during my warfare. Your words give me strength in all my troubles. How they refresh and revive me! Oh Lord, no matter the difficulty, my hope lies in the immutability of Your counsel. You are my shield in whom I trust. You are the source of my security. Your peace will settle over me and calm all my storms. I give all my fears, needs, and insecurities to You. *Goodnight, Lord, You take the night shift.*

I have endured many restless days and sleepless nights. Yes, I knew God had given me His Word and His promises, but I still found myself barely clinging on. I held on to the last bit of hope remaining in my soul! As I laid on my pillow, He began to speak to me in a voice I could understand. During those dark seasons, He reassured me I could trust Him. I wrote down every word He spoke. I read them over and over again! Each day I became stronger in my faith. I held onto His hand during the seasons when I could not sense His presence. I watched God calm my storms.

Prayer: Lord, bless me. I am overwhelmed! Hold on tightly to my hand. Look down from heaven and set Your eyes upon me. I know that You know the number of hairs upon my head. You see me looking up to You in desperation. Don't let me give up! You said Your sheep know Your voice and a stranger they will not follow. Speak oh Lord, for I am one of Your lost sheep. You are my Shepherd. Give me the assurance I need so I can rest knowing You have taken my nightshift. Give me sweet sleep.

> *When thou liest down, thou shalt not be afraid: yea, thou shalt lie down, and thy sleep shall be sweet.*

PROVERBS 3:24

> *Remember the word unto thy servant, upon which thou hast caused me to hope. This is my comfort in my affliction; for thy word hath given me life.*

PSALMS 119:49-50

In My Room

One of the most reflective writings I have ever penned *is this one*. It was so real to me because, as a young person, I always wanted to stay isolated and confined in my room. But there is a danger in confinement. It is only befitting that I leave this writing in its poetic form.

In my room, there is darkness. In my room, there is safety. In my room, there is security. In my room, there is no room for me. I wonder if the light will ever come in. You see, where there is light there is liberty, and I have built such a barricade around me, not even life itself has a chance of getting through. One by one, I jiggle the boards of bondage. These boards of entrapment are difficult to remove! Time has sealed them ever so tightly together. *I believe I'll start where the light begins.* Uugghh! There, I'm beginning to see small rays of the sun. Mmnnn...that's strange! Some of the boards pull away easily while others take considerable effort. Some require repeated attempts.

I soon realize this is a painful undertaking. I sustain almost as many injuries in the process of removing the boards as I did for the reasons I put them up! These boards of fear, anxiety, rebellion, jealousy, anger, hurt, pain, and disappointment has blocked life and light from entering into my room. However, as I remove them, I find they take up too much room inside the room of my soul. So, I must continue to work to remove enough of the boards to create a large enough opening to throw them out of my life forever. But that's not enough either! I must take a calculated risk by deciding I don't want to live in my old room. Do I want to be free? Yes!

Then I must purpose within to do whatever it takes to move out of the place I have always lived *in my room;* then, the Shekinah Glory can enter in and dwell forever.

Prayer: Jehovah-Nissi, I need You to fight for me. I need You to save and redeem me from this Stronghold that has kept me in bondage. Lord, I also call upon Your mighty name Jehovah-Sabaoth. You are the Lord of Host, and I desperately need You to marshal forces in heaven and earth to help me. Please command Your army to fight on my behalf. Protect me from danger and my foes. Let Your light shine brightly upon my path, so I may see which way to go. I need to know the road to freedom. Remove all these boards of defense I thought were protecting me, but they were keeping me captive to my past. *I am ready, Lord. I am ready.*

> *My heart is very pained within me, and the terrors of death*
> *are fallen upon me. He hath delivered my soul in peace from*
> *the battle that was against me…*

Psalms 55: 4, 18a.

HE
HEARD
ME

My Mother's Morning Prayer

My mother taught me how to be a lady and how to be a mother. But more importantly, she taught me to pray. My first year away from home in college, I asked my mother to be my prayer partner. Each morning I rose and knelt to seek the Lord's guidance for my day. *It was a tough year.* I missed home. I struggled to get good grades even though I lived at the library and forsook partying many times so I could study. Finances were always short; I never knew if I would have enough money to return to school after each break.

The entire four years were a struggle. Nevertheless, I never ceased praying. I could not see it then, but God was listening to me each morning. I never missed a school session. I graduated in four years. By the time I reached my junior year, I was off academic probation and making the Dean's list. *Hallelujah!* I knew who I was because the Lord had shown me to me. My mother wrote me letters of prayers and encouragement because she knew I needed to grow stronger and wiser if I was going to overcome life's challenges. The Lord she served was the Lord I wanted to serve.

Prayer: Lord, my life is in Your hands. Show me Your will for my life today. I claim a spirit of assertiveness, with thanksgiving and praise. Don't let me overlook Your plan when You reveal it to me. *Ps.* I promise not to try to figure out Your will. I promise to continue to work while I wait for Your perfect will to take place in my life today.

Lord, my heart is not haughty, nor mine eyes lofty; neither do I exercise myself in great matters, or in things too high for me.

Psalms 131:1

Since I Don't Know

Why is it so important that we pray in the Spirit? It is important because the Holy Spirit makes intercession to God on our behalf with words which we cannot utter. Sometimes we are unable to find words to express what we feel. I had difficulty finding words to express myself. *People say God knows your heart. That may be true, but I desired that He know my voice too.* Just like I wanted to know and recognize His voice amid all the other cries, I wanted to be sure He could recognize my voice in the crowd. It did not matter to me if I was asking for the right thing or the wrong thing. What I was looking for was affirmation. I was wrong! *It does* matter if we ask God for the right thing or wrong thing. *It is* important to pray in the Spirit, so the Holy Spirit can tell us what to ask the Lord for in faith. God knows what is or is not suitable for us. He only wants that which is good for us.

Herein lies the struggle. There are times in which our prayer(s) is (are) in direct conflict with what the Holy Spirit is praying to God on our behalf. *However,* when we pray in the Spirit, He gives us revelation, understanding, and the right words to pray, so our prayers are in alignment with the will of God for our lives. Once I comprehended this Biblical principle, I was no longer confused or living in ignorance. I was now spiritually knowledgeable and able to discern when I was; and when I was not praying in the Spirit.

Prayer: Lord, teach me to pray in the spirit. You said, "and it shall be given you." You said, "Ye ask, and receive not because ye ask amiss, that ye may consume it upon your lusts." I confess I don't know what to ask for, and I don't know what I need or what is right for me. Teach me to pray in the Spirit, so Your perfect will is done in my life. Then, and only then can You give me what You have for me, what is best for me. Then I will be free, happy, and blessed because only the faithful and wise God knows what will make me happy.

> *Praying always with all prayer and supplication in the Spirit,*
> *and watching thereunto with all perseverance and supplication*
> *for all saints;*

> Ephesians 6:18

Praying God's Word

God teaches us to put Him in remembrance of those promises He has made to us. *God is concerned about those things in life that concern us.* For instance, God cares about our children just as He cares about His Son. God cares about our finance. Therefore, He commands us to bring all our tithes into the storehouse. He tells us if we will obey His Word, He will open the windows of heaven and pour out blessings so great and numerous that we won't have room enough to receive it.

God teaches us that a man should always pray and faint not. He reminds us that we are not to get weary in well-doing because we will, in time, receive our reward. He admonishes us again to pray without ceasing, and that the effectual fervent prayer of the righteous availeth much for our labor is not in vain.

God honors His word! God gives us an oath and a promise that according to the immutability of His name, He cannot change, and His word cannot return unto Him void. It must accomplish His plan and His purpose. Failure to do so would imply that He is not God Almighty-Jehovah Elohim. God forbid such speculation!

God declares the former things from the beginning of time. He spoke them into existence and showed forth their reality. He performed them, and they came to pass. God stands ready to blot out all our transgressions and remember our sins no more.

Jehovah God tells us that He is a loving God, and His mercy endures forever. He gives us more grace than we deserve.

Prayer: I Praise Jehovah Elyon, the Most-High God for You are Holy. I Praise You because You are worthy. Your Son is the precious Lamb of God. Bless Jehovah-Yahweh, God I Am. In Your presence is the fullness of joy. At Your right hand are pleasures evermore. God, I shall pray Your word because Your word is the truth. I am so grateful for Your name gives me strength and liberty. When I put You in remembrance of Your Word as I pray, it releases Your power to operate in my circumstances. Your Word is a lamp unto my feet and a light unto my pathway. I will always pray Your Word because You honor Your Word.

Put me in remembrance:

ISAIAH 43:26

THE
FINALE

What about me? What do I Get out of the Deal?

Sooner or later, I believe we all find ourselves asking God the common question, "But what about me?". After we have toiled, struggled, and purposed to do all that God has required of our hands to do, it seems life is still not fair. It seems our lives have more misfortune than fortune.

Sometimes we see ourselves as Job saw himself when he faced calamity after calamity, difficulty after difficulty. Even thinking as Job did saying to ourselves, we have done no wrong, and we don't deserve the conditions or plight we are facing. Indeed, no haughty intention of placing ourselves more highly than we ought. Yet we remain dismayed knowing we are doing our best to obey the will of God.

We realize God is fair. We know God loves us. Yet we are perplexed and, at times, confused. We find ourselves asking a friend and or even asking God, "But what about me?". In other words, it seems the needs of others are met while we continue to struggle. It appears that we are ever meeting the needs of others, but our needs go unmet.

I have diligently sought your face. Yet, I am hurting. I am in deep despair, and my soul vexed. In Psalm 42:5 David said, "Why art thou cast down, O my soul? And why art thou disquieted within me? Hope thou in God; for I shall yet praise Him, who is the health of my countenance, and my God." Then in Psalm 40:12 he said, "For innumerable evils have compassed me about. Mine iniquities have taken hold upon me, so that I am not able to look up. They are more than the hairs on mine head; therefore, my heart faileth me." You would think to be the king with wealth and riches David would have no problems. Such was not the case.

Earlier in the fortieth number of Psalms, David declared his love and commitment to God and even his praise unto God while he was still under attack. He acknowledged the beautiful works of God, and he said we could not reckon God's thoughts towards us. Even if the Psalmist tried to speak of God's goodness, they would be more than can ever be numbered. David found himself praying and crying out to God in distress. David was in a place of drought; a place of bareness, and thirst.

I remember three situations in which that very question, "But what about me?" was cried aloud. I was sitting in the beauty salon one Saturday as my best friend, who appeared to be in good spirits, began to talk about her morning. She was a single mom with a good job struggling to raise her 12-year-old son. There had been an argument between them that morning. She felt she just existed from day to day, staying busy going to work and staying active in the ministries at church. My friend struggled because there was no one to look out for her needs. As she began to discuss the events of the morning, the tears started to well up in her eyes and roll down her cheeks. She looked at me sorrowfully and said, "But, what about me? Who's going to be there for me?".

Yet, another friend who was in what appeared to be a beautiful marriage to those on the outside was hurting deeply on the inside. She was married, yet she felt alone trying to achieve a good life for herself and her children, doing what God required. Staying with a husband whom she knew had been unfaithful, sacrificing all that was within her and seeking God for strength — suffering from humiliation, rejection, and scorn. At her point of exhaustion, she asked that same question, "But, what about me?".

As I pondered their plight, I found myself thinking about my disappoint-ments. I knew I was in a dark place. My husband had not worked a consis-tent job in over two years. We were doing our best to raise two little boys. I felt I was in a failing marriage. I found myself asking God to approve for divorcement. I wanted out!

I can remember pondering and praying to God many times. I don't deserve this. Lord, I don't understand why you won't change my condi-tions. I cried out to God, "Please change my circumstances. What have I done that would cause you to be so displeased with me?"

God chose not to answer me. I was hurting, tired, angry, and confused. I remember driving to work one morning, tears falling down my cheeks, praying to God about my sufferings. I reminded Him *(As if God needed me to recap anything to Him!)* of all I had gone through, all the sacrifices I had made, and I too, said, "But, what about me? What do I get out of the deal?". It was quiet for a few moments, and God said nothing. Nothing at all! Then in a small calm voice, *He spoke.* He did not answer me the way I would have chosen or expected. But His peace settled over me when He said, *"You get me! You get me!"* Then silence fell upon me, and I wept for a while because my heart was full of both joy and exhaustion as I realized I get God, and He does love me.

Hallelujah! Glory to God! God loves me!

Prayer: Heavenly Father, Your love is amazing. Your thoughts are so far beyond my ability to reason or understand. I have come to realize I do not live on an island. So many people need the touch of Your hand and to hear Your tender voice of comfort. Thank You for keeping a watchful eye over my life. You carefully follow me wherever I go. You never tire of my whining. I invite You to orchestrate my life. Bless the lives of your children, for we cannot live without your mercy. We would perish should You turn away from us. I have made excuses not to serve You. I regret the times I forsook You. My heart is full because of all the precious stones and essential people in my life; there is none higher than You. When I am in trouble, I will look up and remind myself of Your words to me, "You get me! You get me!.

Why art thou cast down, O my soul? And why art thou disquieted within me? Hope thou in God; for I shall yet praise him, who is the health of my countenance, and my God.

PSALMS 42:1

Our Special Moments

Aspecial place for a special God, for special times. Thank you for our special place, where we spend special moments for special seasons in my life. You always meet me in our special place. You're never late, never too busy for me. Our time together is very special to You. Our time together is extraordinary to me, also.

Prayer: Father of Abraham, Isaac and, Jacob. All majesty, dominion, and power belong to You. Oh, hail King Jesus, my Lord, and Savior. You are the Son of God who hath sent the Holy Spirit to dwell with us, in us and among us. You are my deliverer and redeemer; my fortress and rock! You are my well that I run to when I am thirsty and dry. You are the giver and sustainer of all life. Oh Lord God, You speak, and mountains move. You **breathe,** and whirlwinds begin to disperse. You stretch forth your mighty right hand of righteousness and sickness; diseases and maladies flee.

You are the Holy One of Israel. You are the One who looks from heaven above and sees the affairs of all humanity. You are the One who judges your creation for You are our Creator. To You, Oh Lord, do I cling too! I humble myself before You with a contrite and grateful heart. I ask You to forgive me of my sins which I have committed against You. Give me a clean heart and a pure mind. I know that all my help comes from You, who hath made heaven and earth. Majestic is Your name. Almighty Lord, as I close this book, our time together has been refreshing. The heaviness I felt is gone.

My love for You has grown in exponential ways I did not know existed. I don't see You the same way. You are real! You are no longer an abstract being in my mind. My outlook has changed, and I feel positive about my life. My mind is at peace. My circumstances have not changed, but my sadness is gone. Oh God, You are my joy and my strength. From now on, when I sense my heart is failing, I will run into Your presence. I will sit at Your feet. I will lay my head upon Your shoulder. I will meet You in our garden. *There in the garden where the birds hush their singing, I too will be still and listen to Your voice.*

> *And in the morning, rising up a great while before day, he went out, and departed into a solitary place, and there prayed.*

> MARK 1:35

The Benediction

*P**rayer:*** Lord, I pray for this reader. Each of these devotions has touched their soul. Many of the words which you have given me to write have pierced their heart. Joy restored. Another is numb. Still, someone else is perplexed. The oppressed got delivered! Yet, another soul found salvation. Praise be to God! You imparted Your peace into the mind of the one once filled with worry. They were not expecting to uproot old feelings. *Your healing power is needed.* A touch from Your hand will restore that which was lost or stolen.

Oh, my Father, I ask You to show every reader how to find their *garden*. I pray that You will make this real to them. I pray that You will meet them each time they go to their *garden*. May they always have a spirit of expectancy. May they always find delight in seeking Your face. My heart desires that they know *You*.

I ask You to reveal Yourself to these readers in a personal way and remove all doubt. Let them know how much You love them and how special they are to You and the Kingdom of God.

My heart is overwhelmed with passion and compassion for these readers. My heart desires that they will understand Your principles and believe Your promises are true. I know each one of these is the apple of Your eye. May they cast their cares upon You. May they rejoice in knowing You and celebrate their relationship with You. May You pour out Your blessings upon them until their hearts overflow.

I ask You to meet them wherever they are in life. You are not looking for perfect people to save. You are looking for the broken so that You can heal them. I ask You to pour out Your Holy Spirit upon them and fill the room they are occupying with Your Glory.

In Jesus' name. Amen.